Television Production:

a Director's Perspective

All rights reserved. No part of this publication may be reproduced, stored in a retrieval system, or transmitted by any means – electronic, mechanical, photographic (photocopying), recording or otherwise without prior permission in writing from the author.

Edited by Moira Burke

Copyright 2015 Rick W. Davis

All rights reserved

"A unique and comprehensive overview of the responsibilities and challenges faced by a TV director. A valuable read for anyone interested in pursuing a career in the 'controlled chaos' that is live television sports!"

>Curtis Saville
>Producer, Rogers Sportsnet

"Rick's concise and informative overview is written with the same enthusiasm that Rick brings to the director's chair on location.
A great read for anyone considering a career in television production."

>Bruce McConnell
>Technical Producer

"Directing is one of the most demanding jobs in television. A good director makes any commentator's job easier and helps bring the feeling of 'being there' to the viewer. Rick is one of the best and has comprehensively outlined what it takes to sit in the chair and make the production 'shine'!

>Rob Faulds
>Commentator, Rogers Sportsnet

Television Production: a Director's Perspective

Table of Contents

Chapter 1	Introduction	5
Chapter 2	Industry Overview	7
Chapter 3	A Growing Industry	15
Chapter 4	A Directors' Day	17
Chapter 5	Broadcasting Education and Experience	33
Chapter 6	Production Meetings	37
Chapter 7	Producer/Director	40
Chapter 8	Crew Positions	43
Chapter 9	Director Pre-Production Meetings	57
Chapter 10	Camera Locations	71
Chapter 11	Camera Specifications	75
Chapter 12	Camera Framing and Composition	80
Chapter 13	Monitor Walls	87
Chapter 14	Director's Lingo	91

Chapter 15	Collaborating with Producers	97
Chapter 16	Cultivating Professional Contacts	100
Chapter 17	Building a Reel/Portfolio	103
Chapter 18	About the Author	106
Chapter 19	Acknowledgments	108

Chapter One

Introduction

Television Directing is a creative career like few others. If travel and adrenalin- filled action sound like something you can live with, then this is the career for you.

I have been blessed with the opportunity to travel to more locations in more countries than I ever would have thought possible: from the far reaches of Asia, throughout Europe, North America and the Caribbean. My life has been about covering professional and amateur sporting events including the ultimate - the Olympics - on numerous occasions. Providing this service for dozens and dozens of companies internationally, I've had the privilege of flying in private chartered aircraft and staying in 5-star accommodations.

I don't tell you this to impress you but rather to impress upon you the real number of opportunities out there if you are truly interested in joining the ranks of television directors. It's a great career!

The electrifying charge you get when you're in the midst of directing a live show is like no other, with your mind so clear you can see and react to twenty different things at once.

Mobile Production Control Room

The feeling you receive from directing is akin to playing sports at a high level. When you're in the zone or when you're truly ON you feel like you're unstoppable.

Your entire production crew will feel it too and feed off your enthusiasm. It's the feeling of doing a choreographed dance when you're all in one unified rhythm.

The buzz, the high, is a total rush that keeps you coming back for more.

In the following pages you will learn the finer points of this exciting and challenging career path. You will discover your next steps to fulfill your desire to become a television director.

Along the way, I'll also give you solid overview of the many broadcast team players that the TV director manages and leads, and what they do.

Chapter Two

Overview

A director's main goal is to give the audience the look, feel and sound of what the event is about and secondly, to interpret and represent the vision of the producers, writers and commentators to the viewing audience.

The director does this by his talent in:
- Knowing the event and players or performers:
- Interpreting storylines:
- Scouting shooting locations:
- Running through rehearsals:
- Placing cameras ("blocking shots") for the best look, and knowing when to maneuver them:
- Integrating crew member input:
- Managing overall the entire crew and support staff.

The director has to do all this creatively, to entertain while informing, and all the while staying as calm and collected as possible.

The director's role during a live multi-camera telecast is that of managing or conducting an entire production crew. Keeping 20 to 30 people on the same page for a few hours is daunting but the rewards of a successful production make the hard work well worth it.

Live Production versus Live-to-Tape

Most "live" productions such as music performances or sporting events are best covered with the use of a large television mobile (see below) employing multiple cameras. The event is captured by the director creating a line-cut of the action. This is achieved by the director giving cues to the camera operators and technical director. The technical director then selects the right button for the corresponding camera to send the image or signal to a recording device.

This coverage style is how footage is normally captured for large events; it also generally comes with a large price tag as well.

The Rolling Production Studio

A television mobile or OB Van (Outside Broadcast Van), as they're known in Europe, is literally an entire TV production facility on wheels. An assortment of cameras and lenses are definitely part of the mobile package. In addition to the cameras, however, is a lengthy list of gear ensuring no post-production work is necessary. This list includes the:

CONTROL ROOM
This holds numerous video monitors fed by all video sources, such as cameras and VTR machines.

AUDIO

This includes the:

Audio control room, with access to a multitude of microphones:
Audio console for mixing the sound:
Audio monitoring tools to ensure the best possible sound quality such as stereo compressors, and Dolby encoders and decoders:
Intercom equipment for continuous communication between all production team members:

VTR

Including the:
Videotape suite, housing multiple formats for playback and recording of all images and sound coming into and going out of the mobile:
EVS machines, which are computer-based recording and playback devices. These units can now handle the work of what 4 or 6 videotape machines used to accomplish. In addition to storage and playback functions they are also used as edit suites.

GRAPHICS

This includes the:

Graphic station, containing computer-based graphic equipment: this makes the titles and full-frame graphics which support the storyline throughout the event:

Video Level Monitoring Room, where all cameras are fed into CCU's (camera control units) to ensure consistent exposure and color-matching between cameras:

Routing and System Equipment - for stable, accessible electronic signals to be transported throughout the facility.

The sound room, VTR area, graphics department, camera control or video level room, and every element you could possibly need for a live production, all exist in this rolling production studio on wheels.

The extensive list of equipment in a mobile easily explains the price tag to rent one for even for just one day. However, if you want multi-camera mobile style coverage without the hefty price tag, here's what to do: you use a post-production facility.

The biggest benefit to a mobile is that you can see all your sources, or camera images at once, and you can see each camera's framing and composition. You can then put together a pleasing line-cut without having different cameras giving you identically framed shots as you create the image sequence.

But if you want that multi-camera coverage look without the price tag, and if you have access to a post-production facility or edit suite, you can achieve the same kind of final results at a much, much lower cost to you as a producer of television content.

Let's talk now about how you could achieve this.

Recording a Show Live-to-Tape

The term "live-to-tape" essentially means the entire production is treated as if you are live on-the-air. Even though the event or production is not going out "live" to a television audience it is treated as such meaning everyone involved must give the production the utmost of attention and professionalism when doing their respective jobs.

So rather than using a fully loaded production mobile, and its hefty price tag, here is another option. You start out by hiring multiple camera operators. Let's say 4 or 5 camera ops for this illustration. You will want to have a full production meeting with your crew. You hold your detailed camera meeting before the shoot begins outlining all of the camera assignments that you expect of them. Where you want them to be, physically in a certain position, the type of framing you require and the style of coverage that you want, i.e., very aggressive quick style of repositioning or always smooth and controlled, from each one.

Many of the cameras may have similar content within their frame because you want them to cover the action. So what you want to do as a way of covering it without a mobile is to setup yourself up in a location close enough to the field of play, with a series of video monitors, that you could receive a feed from all of the cameras. A cable, carrying the camera's signal, from each camera would be run back to you in a director's position. Each camera records, either within the body of the camera, or with an external recording device, their own images. However with the outgoing signal coming to you, at the director's position, you can get a visual representation of what each camera operator is framing. Then setting yourself up with an intercom system, you can be off in the wings or wherever you have all of the camera cables running to. You may want to be far enough away to ensure that your voice is not picked up by the camera microphones.

By using a wireless intercom you can direct your crew "on the fly". So as an example, of covering a live basketball game you may say, "camera 1 – stay head-to-toe with the player with the ball, camera 2 – stay on a shot wide enough to view all of the players in frame, camera 3 – remain on coverage wide enough to include all of the team benches and coaching staff as well as play on the court, camera 4 – stay on just the player defending the ball carrier. Camera 5 – keep the coach in your frame".

By doing this you can get a good feel for how you would like the images to all come together once you begin editing in a post-production edit suite.

Even though you're letting all of the camera operators record everything, for this to work effectively before shooting commences you need to synchronize all of the cameras by aligning all of their timecode. Timecode is a constant internal clock that runs within all cameras. This timecode is accurate to a frame or to one thirtieth of a second.

With the benefit of all cameras being in perfect synchronicity you can edit your shots between the various recordings with far greater ease.

Your on-air talent (commentators) will be on site to record their opening and closing comments. They will also engage with the athletes by doing interviews before and after the event. This is important for continuity.

Once the editing of the event is complete, the commentators are then brought into an announcer booth or studio to voice-over the event as if it were live. The audio engineer mixing the production will use the "nat-sound" (natural sounds) of the sport recording to mix with the announcer's microphones to provide the impression of a "live" performance.

The producer/director will sit through all of the edit sessions working with the editor to supervise and direct the pacing of the cut.

Often times a production assistant or associate producer will aid the director by working from a set of notes that were taken during the event to ensure no details are omitted in the final production.

This gives smooth pacing and the same final result as when a television mobile is used. It certainly takes a lot longer to achieve the same result, but at a much, much reduced cost.

This is a great way to cover large events. I have achieved this method many times over my directing career.

Regardless of when a person enters into the field of broadcasting or how long they are in the industry, one fact has and will remain constant. Despite how many innovative changes are made in the equipment technology that is used, the business of broadcasting is the business of story telling - plain and simple.

So no matter how excited you are about the latest technology toys, whether it be 3D cameras or 7.1 surround sound, a great director will always be a great storyteller.

Chapter Three

A Growing Industry

We live in an incredible age. Never before has so much media content been created for so many people around the world to enjoy. In North America alone, there are over 7,000 television stations. In Europe the number far exceeds 15,000. These numbers include traditional over-the-air stations, cable and satellite networks and most recently technology has led to internet stations. The biggest grand-daddy of them all is YouTube. YouTube offers independent producers of video content the ability to create their own channel to distribute their content. There are also numerous independent stations operated by institutions such as colleges and churches.

All of these stations have one thing in common. They all need content to survive. The business of television broadcasting is like a voracious animal – it constantly needs to be fed - fresh programming.

In addition to all the conventional television stations and networks, we can now add cellular or mobile companies to this list as well. Cell phones or smart phones are all equipped with monitors that will play both video and audio. All of the corporations that manufacture or sell these products are now clamoring to get content to place on their portable devices. And all of this content has to be produced and directed. So if you're considering getting into the business of television production, the opportunities are terrific. Career opportunities for a television director are growing all the time.

In order to get a good feeling for what it would be like to sit in the director's chair, I am going to begin by taking you through a typical director's day. Many areas of expertise and job positions will also be described. Later in the book, I will go into more depth and detail about these areas of television production including the next step you will need to take to get into this creative field.

Chapter Four

A Director's Day

A typical director's day will last approximately 15 hours. This may sound like a daunting task but it's not really. The day travels up a gradual intensity slope with your full energy and focus not challenged until about 10 hours into your day. The last few hours are where the real payoff exists. This is when the juices start flowing, your power levels climb and you get into your zone.

Before we get to the actual day, allow me to give you a bit of background as to what got you to the actual day of the television event. For our purposes, I am going to choose the sport of basketball as an example. Let's take it a step higher and make our example the pinnacle of the sport. I will discuss the pre-production and coverage of an NBA regular season game.

The broadcast rights for a telecast and ultimately the control of the broadcast are dictated by a specific National Basketball Association team. The director is usually hired by the team via a person in the role of executive producer. If not by the team directly, the director's position could also be supplied through an affiliated company which could also provide other services such as technical support. The NBA team could also choose to give the responsibility of all hiring and production decisions to a broadcaster. This could be an individual local station or a national network. At the broadcaster level the hiring will also be overseen by an executive producer.

The complete broadcast team on the production or content side will also include a producer, an associate producer, on-air commentators, a technical producer, and sometimes a floor director.

In the United States the floor director position is usually included on the production team rather than the technical team. In many other countries it works the other way around.

The director is hired usually on a long term basis. It could be for an entire seasons' worth of games. This is 82 games in the case of the NBA running seven months in duration. Or it could be for a portion of the season. The need for a single game assignment will also occur occasionally, often to fill in for a regular director who has been posted to another assignment or may just need a day off.

The broadcast team will arrive in the city where the telecast is taking place one day before the game takes place. Although air travel throughout North America is easily accessible, in case of any unforeseen circumstances occurring, the crew makes all efforts to arrive at least one day early.

Pre-Production

The broadcast day will begin with a production meeting in the morning. This will usually be held at the hotel rather than the sports venue. For convenience and to save time this could be held as a breakfast or lunch meeting.

The agenda for the meeting will include the shows storyline topic and additional logistical details for all of the broadcast team members present. The agenda's content is generally created by the shows' producer.

You may be questioning the need for a storyline since we're talking about coverage of a live sporting event, but this is essential. A sporting event consists of two teams essentially doing battle. Each team consists of many team members and each individual is an elite athlete who knows how to extract the absolute most out of themselves in a game.

The NBA is the pinnacle of the sport of basketball and all the players that compete at this level are truly phenomenal individuals. All of these exceptional players have a story within them. It's the role of the broadcasting storytellers to reveal these tales.

To do well at this level, it is expected that all members of the broadcast production crew will have a good knowledge of the game and the players. Reading daily, and keeping abreast of news and sports highlights on television or internet, is essential components of the job. This information will also be supplemented by a daily news-clipping service provided by the NBA team's media officer. This is a service which will accumulate all team related stories that were published in the various cities that have NBA teams. This provides the crew with all the latest news possible.

The storyline of the day will emanate from all this current information. An example of this could be that one team's point guard had a career game the evening before scoring 62 points. And on the flip side their opponents for tonight's game could have the stingiest defense in the league allowing opposing teams an average of only 86 points a night. Obviously, in tonight's game something will have to give.

The producer will offer this theme as the main storyline – the contrast of two extremes. A show opening, known as a tease, will be written and show highlights of past games inserted to support this storyline. This opening will be edited during the hours of game-day pre-production in the television mobile. This task is usually completed by the associate producer.

In discussion with the rest of the broadcast team, secondary key factors may come to light that should also be focused on as the game proceeds. These additional points can be introduced to the audience as part of the opening on-camera introductory comments by the commentators. They will continue to highlight these points throughout the telecast to support the shows overall theme.

Discussions regarding which players and coaches would be most appropriate for pre-game interviews are discussed. In this particular example suitable choices might include the 62 point-scoring guard and the player given the unenviable task of trying to defend him during the evening's game. Either coach would also work to support the day's storyline.

The producer will outline the day's schedule including a time which the commentators will be needed to pre-tape the player and coach interviews. This will take place at the arena two to three hours before game time.

The television mobile or OB (outside broadcast) van arrives at the venue at least 8 hours before game time to be parked and powered.

Dome Productions Trillium Mobile – Toronto, Canada

The truck engineers lead by the E.I.C. (engineer in charge) will arrive at this time to ensure power is hooked up to the mobile. This power source can either be provided from the buildings power supply or a large portable generator. A generator will only be used when the building's existing power supply is insufficient to do the job adequately.

Next to arrive will be the television technical crew. This is the team of operators who will operate all of mobiles' equipment. The crew will consist of the following positions:

- technical producer

- technical director
- floor director /stage manager
- audio engineer (A1)
- audio assistants (A2)
- camera operators
- videotape/EVS operators
- graphics operator
- video operators
- lighting director

Specific details of these positions are outlined in Chapter 8.

These crew members are responsible for setting up all of the gear including running the camera cables and audio cables and building up the cameras and tripods. They will arrive 6 to 7 hours before game time.

During the hours of pre-production, the various operators prepare for their specific roles during the telecast. The VTR department will begin to assemble the production items that will be inserted into the telecast, including the opening tease.

Mobile VTR area with 4 work stations

The graphics operator will load all of the necessary titles and statistics that will be needed throughout the telecast. This will include opening titles, as well as all identifying player titles.

The audio operators will setup commentator announce positions and install microphones around the perimeter of the basketball court. This will ensure the greatest opportunity to hear the expected live sounds of the competition including the squeaks of the shoes. All of this "natural" sound will become the underlying audio bed which will be mixed with the commentators' description of the action.

The director will have numerous meetings throughout the pre-production stage of the day with the crew broken into various groups, including the technical director, audio engineer, camera and VTR operators. These meetings are outlined in detail in Chapter 9.

When the television mobile arrives, the production area is setup in its normalized state. At this point no camera or tape feeds are going to any monitors. During pre-production the director will work with the engineering staff to setup the monitor wall the way it will be needed to produce the specific show of the day; on this occasion being basketball. Further details of monitor wall setup are discussed in Chapter 12.

Player interviews are recorded usually after a scheduled crew meal break. These interviews can be used as either part of the opening sequence to the show or added during the telecast to help support the storyline as it unfolds.

Rehearsals before going live are usually performed for the benefit of all members on the broadcast team. This will allow the commentators a chance to ensure they're on the same page with each other, as well as give the producer an idea of the overall length of the opening. The opening tip-off is scheduled for 10 minutes after the top of the hour whether the broadcast team is ready or not.

The rehearsal also allows the director an opportunity to check out all the various angles and camera framing that can be used. Tweaks are made at this point rather than while "on-air".

During the last 30 to 15 minutes before air time, the technical producer will check the transmission path with the station or network's master control department. Color-bars and tone are used to ensure that correct and desired signal strengths are reaching their correct destination.

Showtime

This basketball broadcast will operate with 7 cameras spread around various parts of the arena. Some cameras have lenses that can reach up to 100 times magnification.

This allows the director the ability to show all of the action, up close and personal, to the viewers at home.

The longer or more powerful lenses will be placed farther from the basketball court, located high up in the stands. The smaller handheld cameras, with smaller lens, will be right on the edges of the hardwood court. These cameras are light enough to ensure that the camera operators can move around quickly to get the shots that will give the audience the feeling of being right in the action.

As the minutes tick down to the start of the show the director reminds all of the crew members to move to their opening positions that were rehearsed earlier.

The announcers' welcoming comments will be shot live at center court with two handheld cameras providing the pictures. These cameras will quickly reposition to the ends of the court, beneath the basketball nets, during the first commercial break. This will be their game coverage position for the majority of the show.

Although most modern day arenas are lit well enough to provide ample light for high definition broadcasts, the addition of one or two portable lights focused directly on the television announcers provides an additional boost to the image.

These lights are the responsibility of a lighting director, who will ensure they're quickly setup and removed as necessary before the opening tip-off.

The handheld microphones, previously tested, are the responsibility of the A2 (audio assistant). The A2 is in constant communication with the audio engineer (A1), in the TV mobile. If any problems occur a backup microphone is waiting nearby.

As the seconds tick down to the beginning of show the producer and director, located in the mobile, will speak directly to the on-air talent via an intercom system delivering sound into the announcers' earpiece.

Located with the announcers is the floor director, who is in constant communication with the broadcast truck, ensuring no details on the "field of play" get overlooked. The floor director provides hand cues and reminders to keep the "talent" on track.

A script assistant provides a countdown to the top of the clock. "On air in 60…, …30, …10 seconds to air".

The director gives the standby to roll VTR gold and track tape. The "track" instruction is provided to the audio engineer who will activate the fader control.

The script assistant continues, "In 5, 4, 3, 2…"

The director gives the "roll gold" and "track gold" cue and the pre-recorded show tease and opening animation rolls to air.

To ensure redundancy the tape department will have a backup copy of the opening ready to go on a second playback device. Equipment is state of the art but having a backup is a smart insurance policy for any glitches that could occur.

As the pre-taped opening ends the director provides crew instructions, "ready to go to camera 2, with graphics hot", meaning the graphics are in standby mode. "open their mics", a cue given to the audio engineer, "Pan 2", camera 2 begins a panoramic pan of the inside of the arena, "dissolve 2, fly the graphics" the technical director dissolves the sources and the graphics operator triggers the titles to fly onto the screen.

The director or producer will then cue the announcers to welcome the audience. "Cue!"

You're ON THE AIR!

Following the wide shot with titles the talent will be seen on camera.

The director opens a switch to speak to the announcers, "ready on camera", then to the rest of the crew "Ready Camera 6 on a 2-shot with a slight zoom – Zoom 6 – dissolve camera 6".

The announcers introduce themselves to the audience and begin to provide details as to what will unfold over the course of the show.

"Ready to add Duet 1" The Duet is a brand name of the graphics machine which is being used to create all of the titles. The graphics operator quickly changes his output from the opening title sequence to a lower third title graphic with the names of the on-air talent.

The director calls out, "Duet 1 in" The technical director moves the fader bar and five seconds later.... "Lose Duet".

As the commentators make reference to key players, the director cuts between cameras which have been instructed to locate and provide images of these athletes.

During the hour before the game, camera operators provided shots of various players warming up. These images were recorded by the videotape operators. A short edited montage or "bumper" was created to end this segment of the show. This is used to lead the audience to the first commercial break.

The on-air talent is given the cue to wrap up their thoughts.

The script assistant informs the network to stand by to insert or "roll" their first commercial break.

The director continues with crew instructions, "ready to go to bumper from VTR blue with the Duet hot for a blind reveal, ready to sneak in your music" the audio cue given to the A1. "Music in – roll blue and dissolve blue" to the technical director who mixes the sources. The graphic operator activates the lower third graphic revealing the names of the two teams.

The announcers look at their court side TV monitor and add a voice-over to accompany the images being shown,

"…and we'll be right back with the opening line-ups after this short break…"

The script assistant counts down to the network master control to roll the commercial break.

The first 10 minutes of scripted content makes it to air without a hitch. The rehearsal was well worth it. The timing was right on and the energy level is high. Now that the ball is in play, it's up to the broadcast team to keep the audience at home entertained and informed for the next 2-and-a-half hours without a dip in intensity levels.

The director's pre-production meetings now become evident. All the crew members fall into the rhythm of the show and are following their assignments as requested.

The pace of the camera cuts, the selection of close-ups, the use of graphics and the number of replays become a comfortable flow. The director and producer lead the choreographed patterns and the rest of the broadcast team follow suit.

Early in the game it's evident that Mr. "62 points" is picking up where he left off the night before. He has scored 8 of the teams 10 points and doesn't seem to be in the mood to take his foot off the gas pedal. Only 5 minutes have expired on the game clock. Mr. "62 points" runs his defender into a screen being set by a teammate. The ball is passed to "Mr. 62" just outside of the 3-point line. He explodes high into the air and smoothly releases ball. It arches high into the air towards the basket - landing straight through the middle of the hoop – nothing but net.

The opposing coach calls for a timeout. He's seen enough.

The director reminds everyone that the coach has called a timeout and that they're going to take a commercial break. Camera 2 is on the air with a wide shot encompassing most of the players in frame. The director yells, "camera 5 follow #62 back to the bench". Camera 5, who was sitting on the ground at the far end of the court underneath one basket jumps to his feet and starts walking alongside #62 towards his team bench.

A camera assistant, also known as a utility, assists the cameraman by handling the camera cable to ensure the camera operator doesn't trip while framing his shot hustling after the player.

The director continues to direct, "ready 5 – take 5". The TV audience gets to witness #62 receiving hi-fives from his teammates as he approaches their huddle.

"Camera 4, pick up the defender who just got smoked." Camera 4 is the other handheld camera, who has now also run out onto the hardwood court to get a shot of the player who was supposed to defend #62. "Ready 4 – take 4"

The producer, who has been working with the videotape department, lets the Director know that he has two 'looks' or replays to go to break with – on VTR gold and blue.

The director calls out, "standby to roll gold – ready to add your font". Font is the lower screen graphic that the Duet operator has created displaying the current score. "Roll gold and dissolve gold". This last cue is given to the technical director as he pushes the fader bar dissolving from camera 4 to VTR gold. "Add your font, roll blue and under-dissolve blue". This allows the graphic to stay on top of the second videotaped replay showing #62 shrugging and smiling almost apologetically to the camera in slow motion.

"Roll your commercial break", the producer instructs down the phone line back to the networks' master control.

After the commercial break the producer requests the playback of a recorded highlight pack of "Mr. 62" scoring his early points, followed by the pre-recorded opposing coach's comments. After the tape the director shows a shot of the same coach wrapping up his huddle meeting with his players. He then cuts to a shot of "Mr. 62".

This sequence builds upon the telecasts' opening storyline. The production team continues to work hard throughout the next two-and-a-half hours covering all the nuances of the story as it unfolds. The home teams' defense tightens up and Mr. 62 is eventually restricted enough to allow the home team to pull off a comfortable win. The home town crowd goes home happy.

After the game ends there are more interviews. "Mr. 62", now known as the respectable "Mr. 24", gives the usual amount of sports cliché answers to keep the audience pacified. He gives the other team kudos for their strong defense and also gives praise to his team-mates for picking up the slack, albeit not quite enough.

The telecast ends after some final concluding comments from the commentators. They do their best to tie up all the loose ends that were introduced at the beginning of the show and which were discussed throughout the show.

As the technical crew goes into their strike mode wrapping up all the gear, the production team packs up their bags, express their thanks and head off with plans for the next telecast. The crew will either head back to the hotel or board another jet heading to their next broadcast city.

Chapter Five

Broadcasting Education and Experience

The skills and knowledge required to become a television director can be learned through numerous educational programs offered at colleges and universities. Courses in broadcasting, film, radio, journalism, theatre, and general communications are all suitable to ultimately lead an individual to a position in this creative field. Many progressive educational programs will include an internship portion to the overall curriculum. This will allow students to acquire some much needed hands-on experience.

Most broadcasting school programs are designed to offer a good fundamental base of knowledge which will arm students with a high degree of competency to begin careers within the broadcast industry.

Entry level positions in television broadcasting could come from either the technical side or the content conception or production side. Typical entry level technical jobs would include videotape operator, camera operator or junior editor. Typical entry level jobs on the production side could include script assistant or newsroom writer.

Like any craft or skill, there are a number of natural steps you will have to go through to be given the opportunity to become a director. There is no hard and fast singular route to becoming a television director but I will outline some of them.

Transitioning to Director

Given that a director sits front and center in the production control room, it would stand to reason that the individuals sitting closest to this position would have the best vantage point from which to learn or model the director's skill. These transitional positions could either come from either the production or technical side of the business. Jobs that may come from the production side include a production assistant or script assistant who is the individual which aids the director with timing and organization of a scripted program.

Another transitional job from the production side could be that of an associate director or isolation director. The isolation director would only be needed during live sporting telecasts. The "iso" director usually resides in the VTR area and works closely with the videotape crew acting as quarterback for the room. This person will communicate with the director offering the best or most suitable sequence for replays. The "iso" director will also be present during the director's meeting with the camera operators so he or she will have a good understanding of all the camera assignments.

Jobs that may naturally lead to a transition to the director position from the technical ranks include the technical director. The technical director works along side the director following the director's request for shot selections and other visual effects.

Other technical positions which tend to naturally lead to directing would include camera operator and editor. Both of these positions are very creative where the juxtaposition of images is a normal part of their jobs.

Without Traditional Education

Many individuals have entered into broadcasting without going to a post-secondary education institution. With the right work experience and attitude, this can also be achieved. I would caution you however that this is the exception not the rule.

Community cable television is a great place for a newcomer to get hands-on broadcast work experience. These companies are built on the backs of volunteers and they're always looking for eager and willing individuals to train to help them create television programming.

Like most people I prepared for my career in broadcasting by going to school. I attended a college in Toronto, Canada that offered a program in television, film and radio broadcasting. I spent 3 years attending classes and learning about the industry from textbooks and instructors.

I would never knock going to school. An institutional education not only provides a solid base to begin from, it also provides individuals with their first industry networking contacts.

I believe all education is a good thing. Education is growth and growth is what keeps us all moving forward as successful human beings. But I don't think I'm alone in saying that most people grow their skills and abilities by actually doing rather than listening about it in the classroom.

Chapter 6

Production Meetings

Television production meetings will involve all of the key creative and business people involved in the final program. These meetings are important so that everyone knows the parameters that are to be worked within; such as budget, number of shoot or event days, number of crew members involved, number of event locations, etc.

In television the executive producer is usually the network executive who is responsible for putting a production team in place to execute the process of providing the television coverage of an entertainment or sporting event.

This team will usually consist of a producer, director, on-air talent or commentators, usually anywhere from two to four and a technical producer. These positions are generally known as "the above the line" team. In the entertainment field this is a budgetary section which is a negotiable hard cost going into the overall production budget.

Line items which are described as "below the line" would include numerous other crew positions which will be discussed later in this book. These are generally considered fixed costs.

The lead individual on the production team will be the producer. The producer will come in with a storyline that he or she would like to follow. This gives the rest of the production team a starting point from which to set the scene for the day or series. For example, the sports team being covered may have just made a trade for one of the biggest stars in the league but unfortunately had to give up a fan favorite in return. The starting point of the story may be all the great things the fan favorite did for this city, but as the story unfolds, i.e. the game takes place, the director and announcers will lead the viewers along the path to see the benefits of their new star, with hopefully a strong and positive ending resulting in a win for the team with the new player being a central part of the days' success.

This storyline will be supported with the appropriate reaction shots and replays to help complete the picture. You get the idea - the typical Hollywood ending.

Production meetings are a time when sponsorship commitments are also brought to the table. Sponsorship dollars are an important part of the overall television financial plan. Given the exceedingly large size of TV production budgets, working with sponsors to give them the best possible exposure is a win-win scenario.

Creating a good working relationship with the event organizer and media relations officers are essential components to ensure successful events.

If your event is an on-going one such as a regular season game from an established league like the NBA (National Basketball Association) or NHL (National Hockey League) then many of your logistics issues will have been already pre-determined with only minor issues to tackle.

If your event is a "one-off" with no prior precedence then you need to start at square one to ensure all details are taken into consideration.

Chapter Seven

Producer/Director

Many multi-camera live action directors will acquire enough experience and confidence to feel comfortable in the role of both producing and directing simultaneously.

The producer's role within live sports coverage generally involves keeping the broadcast teams' presentation on the storyline path that was outlined in the pre-production meeting before going to air.

This job involves listening carefully to the announce teams' commentary and having an on-going dialogue with them through the use of a talkback system that only the announcers hear. This can provide the announcers with additional support information or possible suggestions of where to take the dialogue, if necessary.

This will also be done through the use of supporting graphics and videotape archival footage interspersed throughout the telecast.

The producer will also generally decide on the timing and validity of replays.

Camera operators will have numerous coverage assignments throughout the broadcast (outlined in detail in Chapter 9). At any given time a camera may have a terrific angle of the sport coverage that will not be used on-air. With a typical team of 6 to 10 cameras covering an event, only one camera at a time can be used on air. This does not include any special effects such as "split screens" which could show a viewer multiple angles simultaneously.

After a particular exciting or challenging play, or after a goal is scored the producer will decide, if time allows, showing the audience replays of the last play or goal.

The replay may involve a second look of the camera angle that the TV audience had already seen but more likely the replay will include 2 or 3 different views that had not been seen but were recorded to tape. Replays are generally played back in slow motion with no sound coming from the taped source. On occasion when the "natural" sound of the play was an important part of the story, then the replay will be played back in real time. An example of this could be the sound of a puck ricocheting off of a goal post.

A producer and director will work closely with one another to get a smooth rhythm and pacing in place with regards to the placement of replays, graphics and other videotaped playbacks.

Many experienced directors enjoy the challenge of both directing and producing at the same time. An associate director or isolation producer working closely with the videotape department will make the producer/director job a lot easier.

One caveat must be stated here. The job of having one person both produce and direct simultaneously is generally only done on sports programs that have a straightforward coverage pattern. This would generally include regular season team coverage with 5 – 8 cameras and 3 - 5 videotape machines.

Any major event such as a championship series that could involve over 10 cameras and 6 VTR sources or any coverage that included elaborate pre and post-game shows would usually include more than one person in these roles.

During a live production there needs to be constant communication with the network or station receiving your feed. This contact, usually known as "live production coordinator", or similar title, is in the master control area. This is where television commercials are integrated into the feed.

On the mobile side the person on site who usually has contact with the network, is the producer. Sometimes a production assistant will perform the phone coordination role if the producer and director roles are being performed by the same individual.

Chapter Eight

Crew Positions

Live television is a team game. It takes numerous people to fulfill all of the necessary production assignments on a production crew.

The television mobile will arrive before the bulk of the production team arrives on the scene. The first crew members on the scene will be the engineer's and an electrician. They will ensure that the production truck is safely and properly connected to a power source.

The first option is to run all the gear off of the buildings power supply, but in instances when there is insufficient electrical power available a portable generator will be brought in to supply the necessary current needed.

During the production setup time all crew members pitch in to unload and begin setup of the gear. Often times everyone will help with things like laying audio and camera cables due to the long distances and overall time that this will take. After the bulk of the cable laying is done, individual crew members will then focus their energies on setting up their own gear.

Here is an overview of all the technical production crew personnel and their job functions:

Technical Producer

The technical producer, the most senior technical position, is the crew chief of the production team.

The "TP" will be brought in early in the planning process of a production. The program is mapped out ahead of time on paper where all logistics are carefully analyzed.

Prior to the event happening, the technical producer will attend a site survey to inspect the venue to get a good understanding of any possible conflicts or problems that may occur on the event day.

Any structures that need to be built like camera platforms or announcer booths will also be determined beforehand on the survey day.

The event producer and/or director will also be in attendance with the technical producer on the site survey.

On the day of the event the technical producer will work closely with the engineers to ensure the mobile works efficiently for the production team.

The "TP" will also work closely with the producer and director coordinating setup schedules and expectations. He or she can also offer suggestions and recommendations with regards to which personnel to hire for specific roles.

A technical producer almost always has worked in one or more of the technical positions over his or her career which gives them a solid base of experience to pull from.

Technical Director

The technical director works alongside the director switching the cameras, video tape recorders, graphics and other video sources as instructed by the director. This can also involve using special effects and computer aided devices to manipulate video images including replays.

This position is also known as the switcher, although the title "switcher" is used more within the confines of station control rooms as opposed to out on live events.

In Europe, and predominately in the United Kingdom, the term "vision mixer" is used for this position.

The "TD" will also monitor the quality of the broadcast images and work closely with the video operators and engineering to ensure the best caliber of image is presented on-air.

The technical director is one of the more experienced positions that is generally held by an individual who had spent some time throughout their career learning some of the other crew positions.

A good "TD" works closely aiding the director. It is a fine line always doing exactly what's asked of you and doing what is best for the telecast. By that I mean that even though a director may be calling for a certain shot to be taken to air, an experienced "TD" may hold of just an additional split second to allow a repositioning cameraman to properly focus the camera lens, or to allow the video operator enough time to adjust the iris of the camera.

A fast action event will have hundreds of various camera shots involved and a good technical director will do their best to ensure each one is properly focused and illuminated.

Audio Engineer

The audio engineer is also known as an A1. The A1 is responsible for mixing the various audio sources, such as microphones, music and effects to provide stereo or surround sound 5.1 audio to correspond with the video being produced. The A1 is ultimately responsible for the overall sound quality and volume of sound being produced.

The level of expertise that is necessary for a top level A1 is quite substantial, given all the computerized software that accompanies the position such as compressors and limiters. This also includes operating and programming the intercom throughout the broadcast complex. A mobile engineer will often assist in the intercom setup but the A1 still needs a solid understanding of the system as well.

The audio engineer position on live mobile remotes, such as a music or sporting event is a high level experienced position. The early stages of this career position would be honed working in studios on more structured news or information type programs.

Audio Assistants

Audio assistants are also known as A2's. Their primary function is to assist the audio engineer. The A2 is often an audio engineer (A1) in training. While the audio engineer is setting up the audio control room, the A2's will work in the field setting up microphones and running audio cables. The A2 acts as the A1's eyes and ears on the field of play. Any problems or potential problems are dealt with by the A2's.

Audio assistants will often work on smaller productions involving just a cameraman and audio operator. Duties involved in this field production work could involve operating a boom pole and a portable sound mixer.

Camera Operator

Camera operators will work in two scenarios. The first role is as a single camera operator, known as EFP (Electronic Field Production) or ENG (Electronic News Gathering) camera. The second role is as part of a team for multi-camera action.

EFP Cameraman on a documentary shoot

When working in a multi camera format, the operator is responsible for all the equipment's operation and the framing and composition of all shots. This will take place while following live action and fulfilling the director's requests.

It should be noted that of all the technical positions on a television crew, the position as a camera operator can be the most physically demanding since the operator may have to hold a handheld camera on their shoulder for very long periods of time.

A good camera operator must have a good understanding of the sport they are covering so that they can position themselves in a location to best capture the action. A camera operator has to be able to work quickly and have a good sense of timing. They understand that they only get one chance to cover an athlete's raw emotion.

Hard camera on baseball coverage

Camera operators are on the front line of television sports coverage. A good team can mean the difference between award winning coverage and average coverage.

Video Operators

The average consumer level video camera has built-in iris and color correction sensors which will adjust the picture quality automatically. However, in fast paced live action, these sensors do not work as quickly or efficiently as a human operator can. Therefore the video operator, also known as a "shader" is responsible for controlling the video levels also known as the iris and black or pedestal levels of all the cameras. They also adjust the hue or colors based on the ambient light color temperature that the camera is shooting under.

Given that the cameras on a live televised event may reposition many times per minute, the lighting situations will change just as often. Therefore a video operator will be kept extremely busy. Typically, an individual video operator will be asked to control no more than 4 cameras during a telecast. This may change depending on the demands of the program but this is a good rule of thumb to follow.

Camera video shading station

Videotape Operators

VTR operators are responsible for all videotape playback and recordings throughout the production day. Some playback material will arrive pre-packaged and produced by the network or station. This might include a program tease, a show opening animation or archival footage to be inserted throughout the telecast. A "tease" will act as a scene set to help set the story line of the day. It will typically be produced using archival footage from past events displaying the day's main protagonists, i.e. the stars of the two teams about to enter into battle.

The VTR tape operator will record all the camera sources, providing there are enough record sources to match the number of cameras being used, and then provide slow motion replays when requested from the producer or director.

It must be noted that the term videotape has become a bit of a misnomer as VTR operators now spend most of their time operating computer based systems which record and store the video images on hard drives not videotape.

One of the most popular of these recording devices in use today is known as an EVS machine or affectionately called an Elvis. The EVS machine has become the dominant industry standard used in live mobile productions around the world.

Mobile VTR/EVS area

Throughout the event the VTR/EVS operator will be clipping or archiving some of the greatest moments of the game. These moments don't have to only be great goals or great saves. They will also include the raw player emotion that is captured on tape.

One of the highlights of a sport telecast is the final VTR department's rollout. The rollout is a culmination of the best and sometimes the worst of the day's coverage. These highlights and lowlights of the entire match or series are presented to the viewer with the accompaniment of music providing a dramatic finale to a broadcast.

This closing montage is where a talented VTR/EVS operator's true talents get a chance to shine.

Graphic Operator

This person is responsible for operating a graphics machine, essentially a computer, which provides all of the text and graphics that are seen on-air.

This is one area of television production that I feel has grown the most rapidly over the years. With the advancement of computing power and new software programs, television graphics are now on par with the latest of what Hollywood uses in movies. This provides viewers with spectacular clarity and terrific entertainment value.

During the pre-production setup time is when the graphics operator will preload all of the necessary graphics. This will involve all of the player's basic biographical information such as position, age, and other biographical information as well as all of the player's latest game statistics.

Given that most graphics machines are compatible with other computers, much of the preload can be done off-site to speed up the preload on game days.

Many of the top professional sporting leagues will provide on-going statistics throughout the game. This information can be immediately accessible to the broadcast team via a computer interface to the graphic machine within the mobile.

Many telecasts will often have a second graphics operator who will operate another unit, which will give a constant score and clock or a mix of other sport specific pertinent information. The units output is usually in one of the upper corners of the screen. The small graphics footprint on the screen has given this unit the affectionate nickname the "bug".

Floor Director

A floor director is sometimes also referred to as the stage manager. This person is the producer and director's eyes and ears on and around the field of play.

The floor director will work closely with the on-air announcers providing assistance to allow them to do their jobs as comfortably and as efficiently as possible. This would include ensuring all viewing monitors and audio equipment located at the announce position is all functioning properly.

This individual must excel in dealing with the smallest of details; things such as set dressing, timing, and sponsor signage. The floor director will also keep a keen eye on details away from the field of play such as a player being attended to by a trainer behind the scenes.

Commercials during televised sporting events in North America is a given. When the action pauses and television breaks for a commercial, it is imperative that the game does not restart until television has returned from break. This responsibility will be given to the floor director. He or she will work closely with the game officials to ensure they're on the same page.

Lighting Director

Lighting directors have a larger role in musical or variety type productions. However if a sporting venue is insufficiently or incorrectly lit, a lighting director would be hired for the event.

Many of today's modern sporting venues are lit with television production in mind. The light levels are generally in the 100-125 foot candle (or 1075-1345 lux) range. This is easily sufficient for good quality television pictures.

Some venues, which come under union regulations, will insist on a lighting director being part of the crew if even a few portable lights are needed for on-camera show introduction.

If a venue is in need of additional lighting, the lighting director and his technical team will light the venue prior to the rest of the production team arriving. Usually this will be done within one or two days before the event begins.

Engineering

Television production is an expensive industry due to the expensive specialized equipment. The gear is in use many days of the year. Each mobile unit will have engineering staff on hand to both trouble-shoot any problems that occur on the day of set-up and production days as well as repairing equipment with replacement parts when the need arises.

Engineer in Charge (EIC)

This is the engineer who generally knows more about the mobile than anyone else on the crew. They will have a good basic understanding of how most pieces of equipment on the mobile work.

Often mobile providers will assign a second and sometimes 3rd engineer depending on the demands of the production. One of the engineers could be an audio-engineer-in-charge, who is assigned to deal only with audio concerns including the intercom.

Chapter Nine

Director Pre-production Meeting

The first step in learning and anticipating the best way to cover a sport or entertainment event is to watch previous examples of the event or similar events. You can't watch too much. The more variety from multiple broadcasters you have the ability to view, the better. You'll see some directing cuts you like and more importantly, you'll also see things you don't like.

Technical Setup Time

The degree of complication of a production will dictate how much technical setup time is necessary for the production crew. Sport productions are produced from mobile rolling control rooms - referred to as "television mobiles" in North America or "OB Vans" (Outside Broadcast Vans) throughout most of Europe and Asia.

Alphacam Outside Broadcast (OB) Van 30

These large tractor trailers can be as long as 53 feet and can expand to double their traveling width when in use as a television production facility. Some of the mobiles are so large that they have to have a second vehicle travel with them to carry some of the production equipment due to road restrictions on truck cargo weight.

Major international sporting events such as the Olympics or the World Cup of Soccer will take years of planning and organization to ensure their success. Venue preparation will often take months of detailed scrutiny to ensure the games have the highest level of success possible.

Many regular season sporting events such as hockey, basketball or soccer will only require a half day setup for the production crew. A typical North American production crew day will consist of 10 hours of work; 5-6 hours of technical setup and pre-production, 2-3 hours of live coverage and 1-2 hours of wrap up.

Many of the newer sporting venues are partially pre-cabled for the convenience of visiting television crews. These cables are terminated at bulkheads near the final camera positions and the other end is near to where the television mobile will park. This allows the camera operators to plug their cameras directly into the bulkheads and then it's just a short length of cable to be taken from the mobile bulkhead back to the mobile.

Larger events and championship series often involve multiple day setups. Any events that cover large areas of land such as downhill skiing, golf, or auto racing will often need 2 to 3 days just to lay all the camera and audio cables.

The director and/or producer may have a very short introductory meeting with the entire crew before set-up begins just to give an overview of the days events, but the real details and crew expectations will be given out as the day wears on. There's no point in taking up valuable setup time with specific details until most of the gear is up and running properly. Given the fact that there are often minor technical issues to be dealt with during setup, the production crew and technical engineering staff needs to put their best efforts into getting everything operating the way it should before any detailed meetings are held.

Pre-production Technical Director Meeting

Once the bulk of the technical setup is complete the technical director will schedule a "fax check" (facilities check) to ensure all of the gear is operating as it should. The cameras all need their tally lights working. When a camera is on-air the tally light goes on. This is a reminder to the operator that all camera moves need to be smooth and deliberate.

The VTR (video tape recorder) operators have to ensure the recorders can receive all the camera signals so that the action can be used for replays.

An important part of the facilities-check is making sure the intercom is working properly. Communication is critical. A typical crew, of 25 or more, needs to have instant access to each other during a live production.

Once the facilities check is complete the director can spend time going over the switching requirements with the technical director.

There may be certain graphical elements needed in the show that require the technical director to layer or "key" some elements on top of others. Split screens have to be created or the use of a DVE (Digital Visual Effect) box may be utilized. This is a method of having multiple images on the screen at one time.

Most of the pieces of equipment that a technical director operates are basically computers or computer driven. Therefore, it is often possible for a director to arrive on site with many of the visual elements or "moves" already created and stored on a portable storage device like a flash drive or memory stick. This can save hours of time in recreating the same "look" over and over again.

The director will also review his or her terminology with the technical director to ensure they're on the same page. It's better to be clear up front rather than waiting when you're into the live production to clear up any ambiguity.

Director and Technical Director Stations
Pre-production Audio Meeting

Now that we're living in the world of high definition video quality, it is easy to think of television as the ultimate visual medium, but the overall quality of the signal is completed by the quality of the sound.

Television networks were still outputting their signal with audio in mono as recently as the 1980's. Shortly thereafter, transmitted audio switched over to stereo sound. And now, television production has jumped to an even higher level. The Olympic Games held in Vancouver, Canada were presented entirely in "Surround Sound 5.1". This trend continues with most major broadcast properties.

I'm a big believer in the fact that great quality sound is what enhances great quality pictures. Numerous microphones must be placed throughout a venue and around the sports field-of-play to ensure that the audio coverage is as full and complete as possible.

As a viewer witnesses an athlete moving from left to right on their television screen, the accompanying sound has to do the same thing. This is only possible by having many microphones placed around the venue.

During your pre-production meeting with your audio engineer (A1) it is essential to let him/her know of your expectations of their audio coverage. Television directing has a lot of subjective qualities to it. If your personal taste dictates that you love to hear as much as possible from the field of play and less of the crowd, you need to communicate this request before the action begins. In a basketball game, for example, you may love to have the squeak of the player's shoes on the hardwood court exaggerated. The previous director who worked with your audio engineer may have had completely different likes and dislikes with regards to audio coverage.

Your pre-production meeting is the time to make these requests known.

Television mobile audio room

Another thing to keep in mind is that your audio engineer may have only one or possibly a few video monitors in his work area. It is unrealistic for him/her to know what is going on outside their field of vision. Therefore, it is absolutely essential that the director keep the audio engineer aware of events going on that may have an audible impact.

Here's a great example of that. At a recent world curling championship, an event where the players agreed to wear wireless microphones while playing the game, one player left the field-of-play to head for a restroom break. I think you know where this is going. With prior knowledge to this happening, the audio operator would have turned off the microphone. Instead the world was treated to the sound of a flushing toilet before the engineer could react.

Needless to say all camera operators, which are part of this production team, are now very quick to keep the "A1" informed when a player leaves the field of play.

Pre-production VTR Meeting and Record Assignments

A VTR meeting is important to ensure that no possible camera images are overlooked when it is essential that they be recorded. It will often be the case that a director will have more cameras at their disposal than record machines, so proper planning is important.

In many sporting events like basketball, hockey or football you may find that certain cameras, usually handheld cameras with shorter lenses, at opposite ends of the field-of-play will have the same camera assignments when the action is in front of them. Therefore the director will assign one VTR machine to cover 2 cameras at the opposite ends of the playing surface. The VTR/EVS operator will switch between recording whichever camera currently has the action in front of it.

Since the VTR assignments determine what ultimately lives on tape after a sequence has occurred on the field-of-play, it is important to keep the playback order sequential as well. For example after a goal is scored, the taped elements that could exist may be:

- 4 different camera angles of the goal being scored
- 1 camera view of the coach and players on the bench jumping with excitement on the bench
- 1 camera view of an elated general manager or team owner in the press box
- 1 camera view of dejected goalie smashing his stick against the net
- 1 camera view of a happy family (wife/girlfriend/husband/boyfriend)

It is important for the producer or director to playback these recorded images in a logical fashion. The pre-production meeting is the time to have this discussion.

Pre-production Camera Meeting and Camera Assignments

During the planning phase of a production all of the camera locations are determined and set. As the director, it is now your role to maximize the placement and investment of the camera equipment.

You must ensure that the camera operators know their assignments, i.e. what you expect them to shoot and when to shoot it. Each camera will have its own assignment. It is a good idea when working with a crew for the first time to bring video examples of past programs outlining the framing you're looking for.

For sporting events, two sets of camera assignments are given out. First off, the camera shots and angles that are necessary to provide the main coverage are outlined. Secondly, but equally as important, the replay assignments are discussed and assigned.

It is our job as broadcasters to try and bring the audience as close to the action as possible. Decades ago, viewers were happy just to be able to watch their favorite sporting event on television. This often comprised of wide angles with the camera seemingly far from the action. With the advance of technology, we now have camera lens and miniature robotic cameras that can bring sports up close right into the viewers living rooms.

Hard camera position for hockey coverage

Camera lens now have the ability to zoom in over 100 times. This allows you an extreme close-up of a persons face from over 100 yards away.

Extremely small cameras, some known as lipstick cams, can be placed right in the middle of the action; even strapped to the helmet of a competitor. Small robotic cameras are affixed to backboards in basketball, to the glass above the boards in hockey and to cable lines above the field of play in football.

When the cameras are in their replay assignments, they must ensure that they leave at least two to three seconds of a static shot at the end of the play to ensure that the director and the VTR operator has time to use a replay effect to exit the replay before the camera has to "swish" or quickly get back to their next live assignment. This is known as giving VTR operator enough "pad" on a replay. There are many times when you're watching sports coverage that you'll notice just as the replay is ending the viewer will see the camera rapidly moving off the subject they were shooting. This is due to a lack of "pad" time on the play.

As technology has evolved consumer television sets have changed from what was considered a normal viewing area (4 x 3 aspect ratio) to a widescreen viewing area (16 x 9 aspect ration). It is important to remind your camera crew that when broadcasting in 16 x 9 that all cameras must keep the main action within the 4 x 3 viewing area so that viewers with older television sets do not lose any of the pertinent images. I'm sure this rule will slowly fade away older sets disappear from use.

Every sport or entertainment performance will have its own unique set of camera assignments. There may be certain similarities between different events based on the restrictions of camera positions within the confines of the venue. A well prepared director will have a specific set of camera assignments for every different event to be covered.

Here is a detailed example of camera assignments for basketball coverage. This set of assignments is based on having seven cameras for the main coverage.

Camera Assignments for Basketball

Camera 1 (located high at center court)

Tight follow play by play, after basket is scored go back to player who scored for reaction.

When a foul is committed, go to the player who committed the foul.
Be aware of substitutions coming on.
You're responsible for benches – players and coaches.
After a great assist go to the player that made the assist, The react from the player who scored will be covered on other cameras.

Camera 2 (located high at center court)

Full play-by-play, stay wide enough to see high cross-court passes.
After a foul is committed go to the player who was fouled (victim).
When at the foul line, include player and the basket.
Be aware of the framing for the "bug" (upper edge of screen)

Camera 3 (located high in corner, also known as the high slash angle)

Full play by play. Stay wide enough to see any players lagging the play.
Look for substitutions coming in and out at the whistle.
You will also be covering the benches for player and coach reactions.
Hero reaction (player that scored) after a basket is scored. (Only if we are not using a low slash position)
Crowd shots when warranted.

Camera 4 (located low in corner, also known as low slash)

Full play by play.
Hero reaction (player that scored) after the basket is scored.
Foul shots – may be just shooter or shooter and basket included.
Be prepared for substitutions coming on and off.
Crowd shots when warranted.

Camera 5 (hand-held located under left basket)

Full play by play, stay wide when play is at your end.
Swish pans (rapid camera movement) are not advised.
After a completed foul shot at your end, stay with the ball until it's thrown back into play.
After a completed foul shot at opposite end, you may be asked for shooter reaction.
Hero reaction (player that scored) after a basket is scored at both ends. VTR (videotape recorder operator) will cut from handheld camera to handheld camera.
Stay tightly framed, after a foul, on the player receiving the foul.
Medium shot on foul shooters (pushing to a tight shot) or you may be head-to-toe zooming out and tilting up to follow the shot.
You may be used for substitutions returning to the bench.
Look for coaches and players reactions on the bench.
On every time-out get into the team huddle, or as close as the coach will let you into the huddle. If a coach is diagramming – let's see it.

Camera 6 (hand-held located at centre court on floor level)

Full play by play, zooming to hero (player that scored) reaction after each basket.
On the opening tip-off you may be requested to follow ball upward for close-up.
You will help cover benches and substitutions.
2 minutes before half time you will be released to go to your locker room drop.
(A "drop" is another shooting location where another cable is available).

Camera 7 (hand-held located under right basket)

Same assignments as Camera 5.

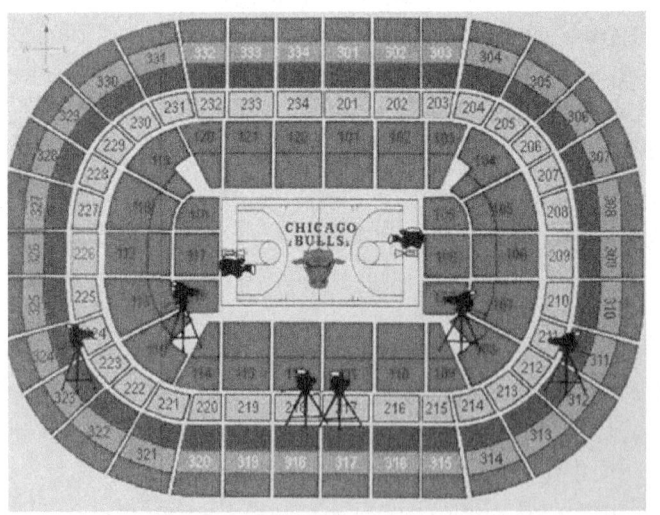

Chicago Bulls United Center – Camera set-up

Chapter Ten

Camera Locations

The proper positioning of cameras is extremely important. This is where the story telling begins. Fair and equal coverage of both teams must be able to be covered from the combined group of camera positions.

Camera locations are often pre-determined in newer professional sporting venues. Architects and designers enlist the services of television consultants to ensure the best and most appropriate angles are considered during the planning stages of these facilities.

Two equally important factors must be considered when determining camera placement positions.

Number one: ensure that television viewers will have the best vantage point to get a true and accurate sense of what is happening during an event.

Number two: ensuring the in-house audience receives the same treatment.

Giving the onsite audience and television viewers the same seat may sound contradictory but it's not impossible with proper planning. Due to advancements in camera lens technology; cameras can be placed farther from the action while still having the ability to get great shots that would have previously been impossible. This ensures that no seats with close proximity to the action have to be given away for the building of camera platforms. The revenue that these seats generate for the sports facility is just too great to be given up without serious consideration.

Hard camera position on curling

Stadium and arena corporate boxes and VIP (very important person) suites must also be taken into consideration during the design phase of sporting venues. These boxes will be the highest revenue earning areas in any facility. The best location for these suites is often at the same elevation that camera platforms should be located. Therefore thorough planning is essential.

Many venues will be pre-wired for television. This means that once a television production mobile shows up on site all that is necessary is for the crew members to plug their truck cables into bulkheads near or at the mobile parking locations and then plug the respective cameras into another bulkhead near the pre-built camera platforms.

If your event is not part of an on-going league that is regularly televised, then camera positions can be a bit trickier. Proper elevations and distances from the field of play are important factors that must be considered.

To get a good vantage point to view a complete shot of the action, the main follow camera should have at least 30 to 35 degree angle of rise from the playing surface.

Before any production takes place, a technical survey of the venue will take place. This will usually involve a technical producer and producer. Numerous factors are taken into consideration on a survey other than just the camera positions. Here is a list of most of the other items to be considered:

- Cable access to the building and cable lengths for cameras and microphones.
- Vehicular traffic paths could be a factor for cable placement at outdoor venues.
- General building measurements such as ceiling heights for lighting or robotic camera positions when applicable.
- Available power and access to that power.
- Elevator access versus stairs for equipment setup.
- Sufficient space for camera scaffold creation if needed.
- Parking availability for the television mobile and satellite uplink truck if one is necessary. Many modern venues provide telecom fiber-

optic lines making a satellite uplink unnecessary.
- Line-of-sight between satellite uplink dish and satellite if necessary.

Once all of the survey details have been taken into consideration then the technical producer will give thought to the specific camera lens that will be needed to provide proper coverage of the event.

Camera Eleven

Camera Specifications

Every sport or entertainment event will have its own unique camera requirements.

Many types of cameras and camera accessories that are used in making Hollywood films have now made their way to television production due to advances in technology. Due to miniaturization of computer related components, TV production gear has gotten smaller and less expensive to produce.

The two types of cameras which are used for the majority of sports television coverage are known as a handheld camera and a hard lens camera.

A handheld camera, as the name implies, is primarily operated with the operator utilizing both their hands to control it. The camera may sit on the camera operator's shoulder but can also be held in lower positions to suit the needs of frame composition.

Lenses on broadcast cameras are interchangeable. The technical producer will make the request for lens length based on the needs of the production and the specific dimensions of the venue in which the production is taking place.

Handheld camera lens sizes are designated by a set of numbers. For example: 20 x 8.5. The first number designates the number of times of magnification the lens provides. A 20 x 8.5 lens would allow a zoom ratio of 20 times to 1. In other words a subject would appear 20 times closer to the viewer with the 20 times lens pushed to the end of its zoom capability.

The second number refers to the width of the shot, specifically the widest focal length in millimeters. Generally from 7.5 to 9.5 is considered a "normal" width. The lower the number the wider the image screen becomes. Once the number starts going below 4 the image tends to appear a bit "fish eyed" or distorted at the edges.

The width factor is important to consider. When the viewing distance from the field of play is not far enough away for all of the play to be viewed then a wide angle lens may have to be used.

Handheld cameras can also be placed on portable tripods to provide increased stability. The base of the camera sits on a tripod plate which has a quick release function allowing the operator to rapidly either remove or replace the camera on the tripod. In live sports coverage it is important for an operator to be able to react quickly to ensure no coverage is missed.

A handheld camera provides the viewer with a more subjective feel than a longer lens due to the close proximity they have with the subject.

Hard lens or box-type lens cameras are much larger and heavier than their handheld cousins. These cameras are situated on heavy duty tripods around the field of play.

These cameras will make up the majority of the camera arsenal on a sports shoot due to the fact that their long zoom lens give greater coverage versatility than the shorter lens of handheld cameras.

The lenses on these cameras typically have zoom capabilities ranging from 50 to 100 times magnification.

The fact that some of the longer lens have so much magnification makes an image stabilization system a necessity to help control the inherent camera shake that is noticed on lens that have over 70 times zoom capability.

The longer the zoom lens the more camera movement and camera shake are amplified. I've had many a camera operator tell me that at the end of the zoom they can see their heart beating on the camera monitor via their hands on the camera handles.

Most sporting events are covered with a mixed arsenal of handheld and hard lens cameras. The only exception to this would be if the field of play is so small that you would not be able to use the benefits of a hard lens. Events such as boxing or a poker competition might fall into this category.

Cameras such as "steadicams" (harnessed to the operator), "dollycams" (a camera on a rail system), crane cameras or robotic cameras are now all common place within the world of television sports production. These cameras can provide dynamic, majestic views of a sport that previously were the exclusive tools of Hollywood movies with their colossal budgets.

One way to immerse viewers into the action has been through the use of extremely small cameras, sometimes called lipstick cameras because they are similar in size and appearance to a tube of lipstick. These small units can be affixed to the helmet of a skier, football player or inside of a race car.

Cameras can also be used underwater. They are placed inside a special underwater casing and can provide excellent shots in diving or swimming events.

Another unobtrusive camera is the pole camera. A small robotic camera is placed on the end of a long boom pole allowing the operator to place the unit close to the action without interfering in play. This can also be accomplished with tracking cameras placed on guide wires above the field of play. An example of this can be seen during NFL (National Football League) coverage.

A Pole Camera at Work

A good Director is always trying to push the envelope to give the audience a new or varied look that will bring a viewer that much closer to the action. Limitations are only set by one's lack of imagination.

Chapter Twelve

Camera Framing and Composition

The elements of camera framing and composition have changed quite substantially over the years. More accurately, it is not so much change but more of an evolution.

It is easy to outline what is considered a well composed shot. General guidelines come into play when framing a subject in frame.

These guidelines are first and foremost keep the subject's eyes in the upper third of the frame. This gives off a natural, comfortable feeling to witness someone framed in this manner. You shouldn't see excessive head room or a lack of head room but rather the subject's eyes staying in the upper third of frame. This rule will never fail you with regards to framing on a vertical plane.

Well composed shot – Eyes in upper third of frame

Poorly composed shot – Eyes too low in frame

The next rule-of-thumb regards framing on the horizontal plane versus the vertical plan. How much lead room or nose room should an individual need in a frame? Generally speaking you should not frame a subject dead center of frame if the subject is looking either left of right. The camera operator needs to allow space, which is known as nose room or lead room in front of the person within the camera frame.

If the subject is in motion, moving across the frame, it is important to allow the subject space within the frame to move into. This rule works for anything in motion; people, animals as well as objects. For example if a car or bicycle is moving within a frame you do not want to have more space behind the object as opposed to in front of the object. This will leave your audience with an uncomfortable feeling as if the camera is trying to catch up to the subject matter. It also makes the viewer more aware of the camera which is something any good director would never want.

81

Proper lead room – Space provided in front of subject

Improper lead room – lack of space in front of subject

Recently improvements have come about so rapidly in the field of camera technology that just about anyone can become a videographer. Whether it's a camcorder, a DSLR (digital single lens reflex) camera, a mobile cellular phone, a tablet, or any one of many handheld devices, anyone who has an interest in shooting and editing video can now do so in a very affordable manner.

This has led to, often times through a lack of knowledge, individuals deeming themselves video producers who are creating videos with framing and composition that has become more erratic and haphazard. Many of the 'rules-of-thumb' of camera framing, that have been laid out here, get thrown out the window as people just basically try to capture the action.

This evolution of camera framing has its pros and cons. The birth of reality television gives viewers more of a 'fly-on-the-wall' perspective of a scene. They are acting as witness to what is occurring in the moment with little regard to how well the image composition is presented. This has allowed the development of a guerilla-style framing and composition of camera work. This is not all bad. In the past the general way of thinking was to not let the viewer become aware of the fact they were witnessing a scene through the lens of a camera. Now, however, quick action erratic camera work gives an audience a subjective POV (point-of-view) of a situation unfolding. They are a witness of a scene rather than a viewer of a scene.

This guerilla-style or run-and-gun style of shooting that "reality television" has made so prevalent in film and television making today is not new. It has been around since the early 1960's. This style of shooting is also known as Cinema Vérité.

Cinema vérité (French translation – "truth cinema") was a French film movement that portrayed people in more natural everyday settings with handheld camera work. In the early days of development this style of camera recording was criticized as being more news gathering than film making.

In this mode of filming, the camera is free to be in constant motion, usually handheld, so as to best capture the scene as it unfolds. This will result in the audience seeing erratic or unorthodox framing and shaky camera results which will include a lack of head room or a lack of lead room. The subject may even completely leave the frame and then re-enter, almost as if the camera had briefly forgotten them.

This style of shooting has its place. It can give a sense of heightened energy and awareness of the action that is taking place. But there can be a fine line between what is acceptable to the viewer and what becomes annoying or irritating to the viewer.

The feeling of zooming in to check your focus and then coming back to normal framing gives the impression that the action began before the camera operator was actually ready to start recording, in other words you caught some reality that you were not supposed to witness. The result is that the audience feels that they are being given a privilege that they did not expect. This gives more credibility to the storyline. You're now receiving the true uncensored facts without any editing, which is ultimately what the viewer wants.

Camera Motion and Multiple Cameras

Another way of capturing a scene or event is through the use of multiple cameras shooting as opposed to a single camera reframing as the story develops. Multiple camera framing will allow a director to give visual variety to a scene. The director can move from an extreme close-up, to a medium shot to a long shot all throughout one scene. This camera blocking can add energy and pace to the production.

Emotion, intensity, drama and a quick eavesdrop can all be done easily through this technique of multiple camera framing.

When using multiple camera coverage a director can experiment with a camera placement that will result in providing the audience with an unorthodox angle or perspective. This break in normality of the camera cuts can add fresh creativity to the program.

This style can make a statement to the viewer that this is no longer just a one-on-one conversation. Now there is technology present as well. For example, an extreme wide shot may reveal lights, grip stands and assortment of other crew members that reveals to the viewer that there is a larger team involved in the production. This may give credibility to the storyline or it may simply be another perspective to allow the viewer to decide what works for them.

At the end of the day, what is right and what is wrong is subjective. The old standards of composition and framing are constantly being tested and pushed to the limits. Reality style also known as guerilla-style shooting and thinking outside-of-the-box has turned camera directing into a new and evolving art.

What's right for you is really up to experimentation. The debate is on. It is never wrong to start with the basics and build your style of shooting from there. It is a sound footing which is tested and true. You decide what is best. Sometimes people can be a little too aggressive right from the beginning and this can detract from the story you're trying to tell.

Let the process evolve. Let your style grow as you evolve with your career. Never forget that camera framing and camera composition is very much part of the overall story that you are trying to tell.

Chapter Thirteen

Monitor Walls

Determining which camera signal to feed into which monitor on a viewing wall is a bit of an art unto itself. With the advent of LCD and plasma monitor technology, a viewing surface can now be extremely large. These monitors can use devices which will divide the single viewing screen into a multiple viewing screen.

Not that long ago, it was considered a luxury to be able to use a quad split generator to split one monitor into four viewed images. The technology now allows for numerous splits, 64 images if you like inside of one large monitor. Of course, every television mobile has a different compliment of equipment. So a director is often limited to what can be made available by the company that was hired to supply the production gear.

Typical monitor wall setup for baseball

It is important to set your field of vision to match the same vision you would have if you seated yourself in the arena or stadium as a spectator. You need to pick a spot from which you are going to determine your viewing access. In other words, if you were a spectator at a basketball game, are you sitting at center court ten rows up from the floor or are you sitting directly behind one of the baskets? Whichever spot you choose as your starting point will determine where your shooting "line-of- axis" is.

For example, in basketball it is generally accepted that the starting point or placement for your main play-by-play camera is located at centre court and as many rows up as it takes to give you a 35 degree shooting angle.

From this starting point your imaginary line of axis or your shooting axis would run from one basket to the other. Therefore you would keep most of your cameras on one side of this imaginary line-of-axis. Using this system to place your cameras will allow for a natural flow of action and will avoid jarring cuts such as having a subject moving left to right on the screen and then suddenly moving right to left.

Once your camera positions are determined the monitor wall will be set up to show provide each camera's picture as a reflection of where they are located within the venue. Cameras that shoot in the same general area will have their viewing monitors grouped together on the viewing wall.

Mobile production companies love the flexibility newer LCD monitors can provide. Given that these new monitors are much lighter in weight than their CRT (cathode ray tube) monitor predecessors, television mobiles can now be made lighter. Some television mobiles have over 100 monitors inside of them. This can do away with the requirement for an equipment escort vehicle and ultimately save mobile production companies transportation dollars.

One detriment to using LCD monitors is that they don't represent colors as well as CRT monitors from sharp angles. The image intensity drops off noticeably as you increase the viewing angle. As you increase the viewing angle, the image will appear as if the black levels are too high and that the video level may be high as well giving the monitor an overall washed-out effect. This takes some getting used to from both the director and the video operator's point of view. I have been guilty of calling for an adjustment of an image that is perfectly acceptable if I had been viewing the image on a CRT monitor.

Labeling Sources

There was a time when monitor walls used to be labeled with pieces of paper and a black marker. However, nowadays titled names can be displayed on computer generated LED (light emitting diode) displays placed below or above all monitor sources.

As a general rule, cameras are assigned numbers and VTR sources are assigned colors. When you run out of colors feel free to choose your favorite animals. And letters can be used for ancillary pieces of equipment like graphic image storage or other pieces of equipment that are available to be included in the broadcast. Some equipment is simply labeled as to what it is, i.e. "telestrator" or a nickname like a "bug" or "jib".

Beside the camera number and VTR color, I also include the name or nickname of the operator. Keep in mind that if your crew is freelance they will be accustomed to having different camera numbers assigned to them on a regular basis so by calling their name rather than number can help eliminate any confusion. Nicknames are fairly commonplace, since on a crew of 20 to 30 people you're bound to have individuals sharing the same name.

Chapter Fourteen

Directors Lingo

The director of a television show has a similar role to that of a captain of a ship. A director must give a constant flow of information to those working around him to ensure that the program (the ship) moves successfully in the desired direction. And when numerous instructions have to be given in rapid fashion, it is extremely important to ensure that those receiving the information completely understand what's being said to them. Clear, concise, communication is one of the keys to being a successful director. There is no room for confusion.

With this in mind, you have to use or create a language that is consistent and to-the-point with every instruction you give. Speaking tones have to be firm and assertive.

As you are now aware, your production crew consists of many people who are listening to what you are saying throughout the production. The crew members will be constantly differentiating the instructions that are for them or for another member of the team. Therefore certain key words will twig with them as being pertinent or not. Here are some general rules to keep in mind when directing:

Rule #1
When speaking with camera operators, if they're not framing what you need instruct them to frame as required or as earlier discussed in the camera meeting. Before taking a camera shot to air always "ready" the camera.

Even if the camera appears to be shooting the shot you want you must always ready the camera first. Otherwise you may find yourself subjected to a swish pan when you least desire it. This is especially important for handheld cameras because the camera may not even be on the cameraman's shoulder at the time you spot an image on your monitor. The operator may be repositioning themselves or the camera for a different angled shot.

Rule #2
Unlike your small consumer digital camera that automatically adjusts your cameras lens for the best exposure possible, broadcast camera lens are adjusted manually by video operators. Although many smaller broadcast lens do have the ability to be put in "auto" mode, this is more applicable for an ENG (electronic news gathering) or EFP (electronic field production) production shoot.

Therefore when you "ready" a camera, you are making three people aware of this: the camera operator who is steadying the shot, the video operator who will make any necessary adjustments to video levels, and the technical director who will "take" the camera to air on command.

Rule #3
When speaking with VTR operators, always **"standby-to-roll"** a certain machine before you "roll" it. Although you may see that the videotape is parked or stopped on the desired shot you're looking for, the operator may be many feet away from the machine at the time setting up another piece of equipment.

When a recording is needed, the correct terminology is "standby-to-roll-and-record". Once the command is given it is usually partnered with a request for confirmation. For example: "roll-record-and-confirm". This two way communication is essential because seldom are the director and VTR operator in the same room.

A favorite saying I have is, "I can't hear the head nods".

Rule #4:
Don't forget your audio engineer (A1). Just because you can see that your handheld camera is standing right beside the lead drummer of the marching band doesn't mean the A1 can see this in his audio room. Before you take this camera you must advise your audio operator that you want them to "track" or listen-in to this camera's microphone before you take the shot. The audio operator may have over 100 faders on their console and you can't expect them to have their fingers on the required faders all the time.

Every director will have their own style of giving out instructions. Adapt what works best for you, but let me give you some examples of situations you may want to avoid.

Be aware of the power of a word. If you decide to use the word TAKE as your final cue, you have to be careful how you use the same word in general language. Let me give you an example of what can happen if you've readied a camera but not TAKEN it yet.

Here's the situation:

During a basketball game, a player is fouled while driving to the basket. You have TAKEN a shot of the player with camera 1 showing a discussion with another teammate before heading to the foul line to shoot his foul shot.

You are preparing Camera 3 that you want this camera to start on a head-to-toe shot of the player at the foul line and then pull out to allow the viewer to see the ball heading towards the basket.

As you were preparing Camera 3 with these instructions, the coach from the offending foul team decides to substitute two players. The two players who are leaving the floor head to the bench but one walks to the left and one walks to the right of the bench.

During your camera meeting you've already discussed with Camera 4 that one of their assignments would be to follow players off during substitutions, so you notice on your monitor wall that Camera 4 is on a wide shot showing the two players leaving. A graphic is ready to be used stating how many fouls the offending player now has. You quickly instruct Camera 4 to TAKE the player walking towards the right end of the bench. What has happened?

Even though just seconds before you had readied camera 3 for the foul shot, Camera 4 is now on air because you used Camera 4 and the word TAKE in the same sentence.

A much better instruction would have been Camera 4 "follow", or "stay with" as opposed to TAKE the player on the right. This is a simple choice of words with a very different outcome.

Using simple words and language inflection can be enough to get the technical director and director on the same page. It helps to place emphasis on the word TAKE when using it to aid in the process.

Years ago before I became a director I worked as a technical director. It was then that I began to create my own style based on what I didn't like hearing from other directors as much as what I liked. For example, I was never a big fan of the finger snap in my ear. One particular director would ready a camera and then simply snap his fingers instructing me beforehand that the finger snap was my cue to TAKE the camera to air. I really didn't enjoy this as I started to feel like a trained monkey at a zoo.

Another example I'm not a big fan of is to simply say the word TAKE as the final command. For example, ready 3, ready 4, ready 2 TAKE. The technical director would be expected to TAKE camera 2. Although this is very clear and concise I prefer yelling out the final number i.e. - ready 3, ready 4, ready 2, TAKE 2!

All styles certainly have room for error and I guarantee that sometimes mistakes will occur. All errors are difficult to eradicate given the speed at which we do our jobs but the key is to try to minimize the risks whenever possible. This is done by meticulous preparation in the form of good pre-production meetings with all the various crew members.

Here's another word of caution to a director. Don't become a spectator. It is easy to get caught up in an interesting game and to just start watching TV. Sometimes an individual athlete's performance holds an entire audience spellbound as they perform their magic on a given day. Take care not to get caught in their spell.

Chapter Fifteen

Collaborating with the Producer

In television sports the production team is led by a group including the producer, director and on-air commentators. It's the producer's job, often in collaboration with on-air announcers, to come up with a storyline that they would like to introduce to the viewing audience as a starting point for the day's telecast.

The storyline commences with the show opening or "tease". This piece of videotape informs the audience of what they can expect to see on the upcoming program. It may pit one team's top player versus the other team's top player.
Now often times "real life" has a way of rewriting the best of intentions so sometimes the so-called storyline has to be thrown out the window or drastically altered to make sense of what is currently taking place on the field of play.

The relationship between the producer and director will often have a choreographed feel to it. Both sides need to have the ability to take the lead at certain times. The producer will have a collection of material that is earmarked to be inserted into the show as the game unfolds and as the storyline dictates. The producer will also be watching the videotape monitors to determine which angles of action may be best suited for replays.

After a natural pause in live action, the producer will call for a replay to be taken from one in a series of VTR machines. The director will insert the recorded replays and then go back to the live game action.

Both the producer and director will listen closely to the announcers and try to support their commentary with appropriate images. The director will do this with live shots and the producer may do this by requesting the VTR department to edit together a series of shots from the event or to standby archive material to support the voice track.

Production Team

Crew selection is a very important factor for a successful telecast. It is a given that all the broadcast team members must be competent at their given skill but the intangible factor is how well the various individuals all get along as a team. This can be a challenge when considering that a full crew with support staff may be over 40 in number.

Producers and directors all have their favorites so it's important when creating a crew to collaborate to ensure they're putting an effective and productive unit together.

Having some redundancy within the crew is also an important factor. Emergencies will arise. Trust me. Whether it's someone getting ill onsite or if a crew member has to suddenly depart due to serious family issues, as a team leader you need to be prepared.

I have found myself in foreign countries where speaking the local language was a challenge. When a crew member suddenly had to leave us for personal reasons we were covered with a backup. We simply moved a crew member from one position to another because they had the necessary experience. From a budgetary point of view this may seem to be a luxury at times but it's not. An experienced crew with depth will always prove to be an asset in the long run.

Chapter Sixteen

Cultivating Professional Contacts

A great production comes to an end; cue and roll the closing animation, add an inspiring roll-out montage with dramatic music, add a copyright graphic and then fade to black.

High fives and handshakes are all around.

When working as a freelancer you must be aware of the fact that once your event comes to an end, it's very easy for your employer - whether that be a network or an independent production company - to lose track of you.

Through my own experience, I can assure you that success is very achievable working as a freelancer in the broadcasting industry. Whether you're setting out as a director, producer or any other key position in this exciting industry, a self-employed position awaits you if you choose. As with any independent career, perseverance and some smart strategies go a long way.

Assuming you did a great job on your last assignment you must be aware of the fact that those that hired you are on to their next big challenge. That could be a completely different sport or a completely different genre.

It is very important to be constantly updating your contact lists and keeping your business associations current and "in-touch". Networking with other industry professionals is essential.

With the advent of numerous social networking groups such as LinkedIn, Facebook and Twitter, staying connected has never been easier. Even the process of signing up for these services is beneficial for you because it forces you to focus on your career accomplishments as a requirement of setting up your homepages.

The concept of "six degrees of separation" comes to mind when you think of networking. This widely held belief states that everyone is at most only six steps, or six relationships, away from one another.

The very nature of the broadcast business allows for global networking opportunities. My career as a television director allows me the opportunity to meet and work closely with other broadcasters at international championships. This is a great way to dissolve geographical limitations.

A wonderful byproduct of networking on an international level is that it allows you to see numerous other societies and their cultural differences. From a creative point of view, the more breadth and experience you are immersed in, the better it will be for your craft.

You may think of yourself as a "sports director" or "music video director" but it's amazing how new opportunities will present themselves to you when you keep your name, face and voice in front of others.

Networking is not always easy, but it is essential to do if you want to receive guaranteed results. As our friends at Nike say, "Just Do it".

Chapter Seventeen

Building a Reel/Portfolio

A reel or portfolio is a compilation or highlight roll of the "best of you". Treat it with respect and something to be proud of.

As you gather more experience in your career, it is essential that you keep adding to and revising your portfolio reel with your latest experiences. Television production is an audible and visual medium therefore it is necessary to be able to provide any potential employer with examples of how your creativity is portrayed on screen.

Experience will come from various genres and it is important for potential employers to get a good sense of your assorted experiences. You may never know if one of your many gigs over the years may twig with someone looking to use your services.

"Early in your career" has numerous meanings. You should consider your days learning in school, as well as any volunteer time you donate as part of your career.

If you have felt pride in any of your early accomplishments then you should consider the project worthy of your portfolio. As the overall size of your reel/portfolio grows, you'll become more selective with what you want to present to each potential employer.

It is important to target your reel to the company you're pitching it to. The same way you may highlight certain aspects of a resume, the same holds true for your "demo reel".

You don't want to be running into an edit suite every time you're looking to apply for a career job. This could be a costly endeavor. But when you are in the edit suite, consider putting together a few versions of your reel. For example you could create a "sport reel", an "entertainment reel" and a "documentary reel".

Never lose sight of the fact that you are in the entertainment industry. The story may be the meat of the matter but it's the sizzle that sells. Keep your reel accurate and entertaining. If you don't possess the necessary editing skills to produce a top notch portfolio reel then hire someone that does. It will be worth it to you in the end. There's no room whatsoever for a typo or missed flash frame. Inform, entertain and be brief.

Diversity is important but as your career lengthens you will have multiple examples from the same genre. You may want to reduce some examples and showcase only the best or newest to your potential employer.

Don't forget written letters of praise as well, whether it's a short email or a glowing letter of recommendation written on a company's letterhead. Potential employers will want to hear about these details. These written commendations can easily be imported into a format that can be used within the body of your video reel/portfolio.

It's easy to stop thinking about your "demo reel". When your career is humming along nicely take a pause from all the kudos and force yourself to think about updating your portfolio. Not only will this accomplish the task at hand, but the fact things are going well at the time will allow you to be even more aware of some of your best work which will be worthy of adding to your reel.

Things in industry can change in a heartbeat. Even though you may feel you are a great asset to your company, budgets can be slashed, sponsors can pull out and a network executive may decide to take a new tack. All televised shows and event coverage eventually end.

Remember the Boy Scout motto – "Always Be Prepared"!

Chapter Eighteen

About the Author - Rick W. Davis

Multiple award-winning producer/director, Rick Davis, has been working in the television broadcast industry for over 30 years. Although Rick works primarily in the sports genre, he has also garnered attention for his documentary work and efforts with charitable organizations.

He has produced and/or directed at numerous international sporting events including the Olympics, Pan American and Commonwealth Games, FIFA World Cup soccer and several other world championships.

He has been a key contributor to the early development of 3 national television sports networks. His services and mentorship have helped fledgling industry people to grow and understand the challenges of this dynamic industry.

In 2006 Rick was presented with an industry award for raising awareness of the importance for early childhood education in the Caribbean country of Jamaica. The documentary, "Jamaican Proud", was produced to showcase the work of North American assistance for the island's future leaders through educational assistance.

In 2008, Rick was presented with Dressage Canada Media Award for the outstanding coverage given to the 2008 Olympic Games in Hong Kong.

In 2012 Rick was part of the broadcast team that again won for their Olympic equestrian coverage from the London Olympics.

Rick is married and has two sons. He resides near Toronto, Canada.

Chapter Nineteen

Acknowlegments

The author would like to graciously thank the following individuals for their help and support in helping to make this book possible:

Moira J. Burke
Editor
For her many tireless hours of proof-reading and her countless words of support and encouragement.

Mike Johnson
Mobile Television Engineer
For the use of his photographs

Al Karloff
Mobile Television Engineer
For the use of his photographs

That's a wrap!

Printed in Great Britain
by Amazon